What Would It Be Like?

by

McArthur Krishna

Illustrations by
Ayeshe Sadr &
Ishaan Dasgupta

Little Adventures is an imprint of Amberjack Publishing

Amberjack Publishing
228 Park Avenue S #89611
New York, NY 10003-1502
http://amberjackpublishing.com

Publisher's Cataloging-in-Publication data

Krishna, McArthur, author
Sadr, Ayeshe, illustrator
Dasgupta, Ishaan, illustrator.

What Would It Be Like? / By McArthur Krishna
Illustrated by Ayeshe Sadr & Ishaan Dasgupta.

New York [New York] : Amberjack Publishing, 2016.
Series : Little Adventures.

ISBN 978092587218
LCCN 2015958566.

Summary: With real-life examples of women from
a wide range of walks of life, girls learn they can do
anything.

LCSH: Women—Biography—Juvenile literature.
Women—History—Juvenile literature.

Women heroes--Biography--Juvenile literature.
BISAC: JUVENILE NONFICTION / Biography &
Autobiography / Women.

LCC: CT3207 .K75 2016
DDC: 920.72—dc23.
Printed in the United States of America

Howdy Adventurers!

Here's the thing – you can be anything you want! But the best thing you can be is you.

Make sure to flip to the Adventure Page in the back of the book to learn more about each woman and her real-life adventures!

Your friend,
McArthur

An adventurous girl once wondered,
"What would it be like. . . to be a cowgirl?"

To twirl a lasso roping the steers?
To gallop the plains on a painted pony?
To curl up with cows under sparkling stars
whistling campfire songs?

She wanted to know. . .
So she went to the library,
where she learned about
*Sandra Day O'Connor**
Yeediggedog!

A dashing girl once wondered,
"What would it be like... to be a pirate?"

To sail the seas through mermaid songs
and barking seals?
To swing aboard with a cutlass
clenched in your teeth?
To fire the cannons
and steal the treasure chest?

She wanted to know. . .
So she went to the library,
where she learned about
*Jacquotte Delahay**
Ahoy, matey!

A confident girl once wondered,
"What would it be like. . . to be the president?"

To listen all day, puzzling and mulling
and chewing on thoughts to solve big problems?
To lead people by serving them
and promoting liberty for all to make life choices?
To visit far-off lands
so people know we are all one world together?

She wanted to know. . .
So she went to the library,
where she learned about
many women who have led their countries!*
Let's serve!

An energetic girl once wondered,
"What would it be like. . . to be a chemist?"

To dream up new ideas about how
space and time and light beams work?
To fiddle with batteries and coils and tangent galvanometers
and energy transfer apparatus and density rods?
To set up experiments to see
what might happen if we try this. . . ?

She wanted to know. . .
So she went to the library,
where she learned about
*Marie Skłodowska Curie**
Eureka!

11

A dazzling girl once wondered,
"What would it be like. . . to be a trapeze artist?"

To sparkle in a shimmery leotard
waving from a board so high in the sky?
To leap into the air for a layout with a flip
or dangle from the bar for a backend straddle?
To feel the grip of the catcher's hands
and come up with a smile to fly freely again?

12

She wanted to know. . .
So she went to the library,
where she learned about
*Antoinette Concello**
Lista!

A brave girl once wondered,
"What would it be like... to be an astronaut?"

To buckle up tight and go for a wild ride
through atmosphere and stars?
To land on the moon
and bounce about with zero gravity?
To turn and see home sweet home,
Earth, from 238,855 miles away?

14

She wanted to know. . .
So she went to the library,
where she learned about
Mae Carol Jemison*
Roger that!

A creative girl once wondered,
"What would it be like. . . to be a writer?"

To play with words
and make them spin
and twirl and hop?
To weave tales of fancy
and delight?
To create new worlds
and people who do
jumping jacks
or love strawberries
or ride elephants—
or anything else you wish!

She wanted to know. . .
So she went to the library,
where she learned about
Isabel Allende*
Word!

17

To look down your rifle
and squint your eye?
To aim so true that you could
snuff out a candle with one sure shot?
To shoot so fast and true
you could hit dimes tossed in the air?

She wanted to know. . .
So she went to the library,
where she learned about
Annie Oakley*
Bullseye!

An ambitious girl once wondered,
"What would it be like. . .
to be a businesswoman millionaire philanthropist?"

To solve problems with a brand new thing-a-ma-jig?
To have thousands of people want to buy your new thing?
To make a lot of jobs for people
and give money to help many, many more?

She wanted to know. . .
So she went to the library,
where she learned about
Madame C.J. Walker*

You can do it!

A bold girl once wondered,
"What would it be like. . .
to be a spy?"

To sneak and snoop and slink around
trying to find information to share?
To be so passionate
you risk your life to help others?
To play with danger as if it were a game?

She wanted to know. . .
So she went to the library,
where she learned about
Virginia Hall*
Shh...

A loving girl once wondered,
"What would it be like. . .
to be a Mom?"

To choose to bring a soul into the world
and teach them to be kind?
To snuggle and kiss their booboos
and sing to them at night?
To love them no matter what, through happiness,
sadness, mischievousness, and madness.

She wanted to know. . .
So she went to the library,
where she learned about
*mothers everywhere**
Love you!

A determined girl once wondered,
"What would it be like... to be an activist for peace?"

To know without a doubt
that people need freedom?
To march boldly in parades
and give fiery speeches
to demand rights for all?
To never give up,
though put in prison
and separated from your family?

26

She wanted to know. . .
So she went to the library,
where she learned about
*Aung San Suu Kyi**
Don't live in fear!

A curious girl once wondered,
"What would it be like. . . to be an explorer?"

28

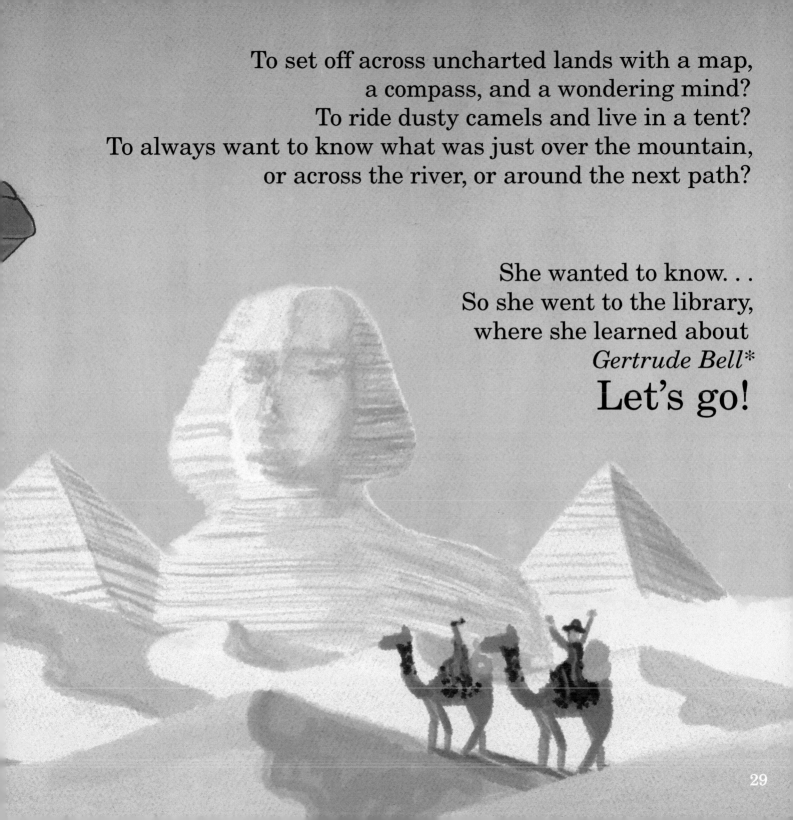

To set off across uncharted lands with a map,
a compass, and a wondering mind?
To ride dusty camels and live in a tent?
To always want to know what was just over the mountain,
or across the river, or around the next path?

She wanted to know. . .
So she went to the library,
where she learned about
*Gertrude Bell**
Let's go!

A true girl once wondered,
"What would it be like. . . to be herself?"

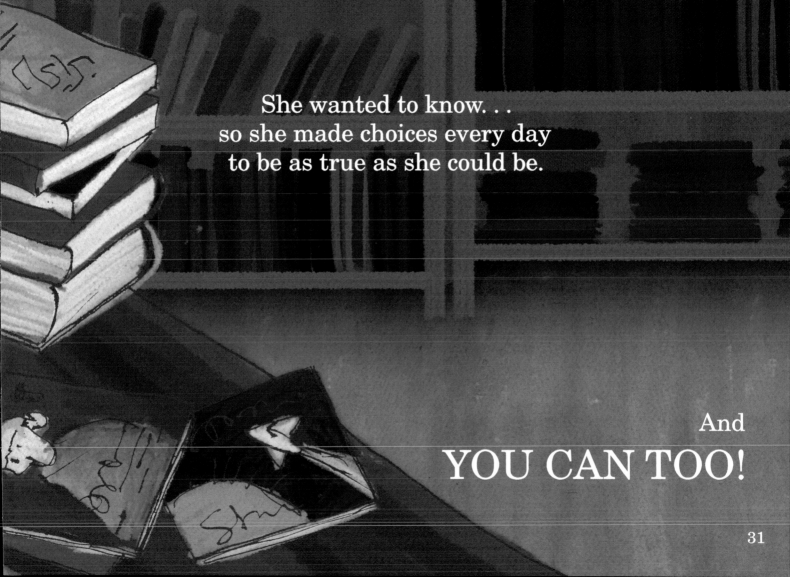

She wanted to know. . .
so she made choices every day
to be as true as she could be.

And

YOU CAN TOO!

Adventure Page

*Page 5: **Sandra Day O'Connor** grew up on her family's Lazy B Ranch in Arizona. She rode horses, shot guns, and worked with the cattle on the ranch. She became the first female Supreme Court Justice of America.

*Page 7: **Jacquotte Delahaye** led a gang of hundreds of pirates that even took over a small island in the Caribbean in 1656. She faked her own death but became known as "Back from the Dead Red" because of her striking red hair.

*Page 9: Many women have led their own country— here are a few: Margaret Thatcher (England), Indira Ghandi (India), Vigdís Finnbogadóttir (Iceland), and Chandrika Kumaratunga (Sri Lanka) were all the "Head of State" in their country.

*Page 11: **Marie Skłodowska Curie** was a Polish scientist and inventor who struggled to go to school because she was a girl. She was the first woman to win the Nobel Prize and only person to win twice in different science fields.

*Page 13: **Antoinette Concello** was called the "greatest woman flyer of all time." In 1928, she left her convent school and joined the circus. She was the first female trapeze artist to complete the dangerous triple somersault and performed with the world famous Ringling Brothers Barnum and Bailey Circus.

*Page 15: **Mae Carol Jemison** is a doctor, astronaut, and dancer! As the first African American female astronaut, Jemison went into orbit on board the Space Shuttle named Endeavor.

*Page 17: **Isabel Allende** is a Chilean-American poet and author. She has received an award for contributing "to the beauty of the world" with stories of magical realism. She has sold over 56 million books in 30 languages.

*Page 19: **Annie Oakley** was a sharpshooter hunter from an early age in order to feed her family. When she performed, she set many records and delighted audiences. At about 90 feet she could split a playing card in half—with the skinny edge facing her!

*Page 21: **Madam C. J. Walker** was born a child of slaves and she had to work very hard as a washerwomen. Then she launched a hair care and cosmetic business and became the first female self-made millionaire in America. She gave awards to her employees for both who had earned the most AND who had given away the most to charity.

*Page 23: **Virginia Hall** was a spy in WWII for both the British and the Americans—the Germans called her the "most dangerous of all spies." Virginia pretended to be a journalist working for a newspaper. Once, she escaped across the mountains by foot—a feat, because Virginia had an artificial foot with the codename Cuthburt.

*Page 25: Many of us have a mother, and each mother is different, just like you are different from any other person. What has your mother done for you today?

*Page 27: **Aung San Suu Kyi** was determined to help her people of Burma gain democracy. She led marches and gave a talk to half a million people. The army arrested her and she lived under house arrest for fifteen years. She was awarded the Nobel Peace Prize.

*Page 29: **Gertrude Bell** was an archeologist, political advisor, mountaineer, and writer. She spoke Arabic, Persian, French, and German fluently. She became such a friend to the different tribes and leaders that they referred to her as "al-Khatun" (or a Lady of the Court).

*Page 31: **You.** There is only one of you – and the best gift you can give the world is to be your truest self.
Be you.
Love, McArthur